THE BALLAD OF THE
HARP-WEAVER

THE BALLAD OF THE
HARP-WEAVER

Edna St. Vincent Millay

ILLUSTRATED BY
Beth Peck

PHILOMEL BOOKS • NEW YORK

To Emma Eve and Emma Millar

"The Ballad of the Harp-Weaver" by Edna St. Vincent Millay.
Copyright © 1922, 1950 by Edna St. Vincent Millay. Reprinted
by arrangement with Elizabeth Barnett, Literary Executor.
Illustrations copyright © 1991 by Beth Peck.
"About the Poet" copyright © 1991 by Elizabeth Barnett.

Published by Philomel Books,
a division of The Putnam & Grosset Book Group,
200 Madison Avenue, New York, NY 10016.
Published simultaneously in Canada
Printed in Hong Kong by South China Printing Co. (1988) Ltd.
Calligraphy by David Gatti
The text was set in Breughel 55

Library of Congress Cataloging-in-Publication Data
Millay, Edna St. Vincent, 1892–1950. The ballad of the harp weaver / by Edna St. Vincent
Millay.   p.   cm.   Summary: A picture book version of the Millay poem depicting the close
relationship between a young boy and his mother.   ISBN 0-399-21611-1 : 1. Children's
poetry, American.   [1. Mothers and sons—Poetry. 2. American poetry.]   I. Title.
PS3525.I495B3   1991   811'.52—dc20   90-19712   CIP   AC
First Impression

About the Poet

She was born in 1892, on February 22nd—Washington's birthday. She was tiny and red-haired. Family and friends called her Vincent. To the many readers of her poetry, she is Edna St. Vincent Millay.

Vincent grew up in the small town of Camden, Maine, by the sea, with her two younger sisters, Norma and Kathleen, and their mother, Cora. When Vincent was eight, her parents divorced. Henry Millay, her father, was a high school teacher and school superintendent, but he was also a gambler with irresponsible ways. And so Cora Millay took on the care of her daughters herself. To support them, she became a practical nurse.

Despite the absence of a husband and father, life for the four Millays was full of joy, high spirits, and many interests. The fact that their mother was often away from home round-the-clock, tending sick patients, drew the three sisters close together. With Vincent in charge, they made housekeeping chores into games—sometimes adding a merry tune to cheer themselves on. One favorite was a song Vincent wrote to wash dishes by called "I'm the Queen of the Dishpan, hurray!" Money was scarce, but Cora Millay, who had been a singer and loved literature, saw to it that her girls had wonderful books, piano and singing lessons, and pretty ribbons for their hair. "Although we sometimes did without a few of life's necessities," Edna Millay later recalled, "we rarely lacked for its luxuries."

Above all, Cora Millay encouraged and inspired her daughters to express themselves and to be creative: Kathleen became a writer; Norma, an actress and a singer; Vincent, one of America's greatest lyric poets.

Long after her childhood days on the coast of Maine, when she was grown and famous and living in Paris, Vincent would write her mother: "I have never met anybody in my life, I think, who loved his mother as much as I love you. I don't believe there ever was anybody who did, quite so much, and quite in so many wonderful ways . . . the reason I am a poet is entirely because you wanted me to be and intended I should be, even from the very first. You brought me up in the tradition of poetry, and everything I did you encouraged. I can not remember once in my life when you were not interested in what I was working on, or even suggested that I should put it aside for something else."

In a later letter to Cora, she enclosed a copy of her poem "The Ballad of the Harp-Weaver" with these words: "I hope you will like this poem, darling. It is dedicated to you, of course, as may be seen at first glance. Much love, mother dear, —Vincent."

Elizabeth Barnett, Literary Executor
Steepletop, Autumn 1990

"Son," said my mother,
   When I was knee-high,
"You've need of clothes to cover you,
   And not a rag have I.

"There's nothing in the house
   To make a boy breeches,
Nor shears to cut a cloth with,
   Nor thread to take stitches.

"There's nothing in the house
   But a loaf-end of rye,
And a harp with a woman's head
   Nobody will buy."
   And she began to cry.

That was in the early fall.
    When came the late fall,
"Son," she said, "the sight of you
    Makes your mother's blood crawl,—

"Little skinny shoulder-blades
    sticking through your clothes!
And where you'll get a jacket from
    God above knows.

"It's lucky for me, lad,
    Your daddy's in the ground,
And can't see the way I let
    His son go around!"
    And she made a queer sound.

That was in the late fall.
    When the winter came,
I'd not a pair of breeches
    Nor a shirt to my name.

I couldn't go to school,
    Or out of doors to play.
And all the other little boys
    Passed our way.

"Son," said my mother,
   "Come, climb into my lap,
And I'll chafe your little bones
   While you take a nap."

And, oh, but we were silly
   For half an hour or more,
Me with my long legs
   Dragging on the floor,

A-rock-rock-rocking
   To a mother-goose rhyme!
Oh, but we were happy
   For a half an hour's time!

But there was I, a great boy,
   And what would folks say
To hear my mother singing me
   To sleep all day,
   In such a daft way?

Men say the winter
    Was bad that year;
Fuel was scarce,
    And food was dear.

A wind with a wolf's head
    Howled about our door,
And we burned up the chairs
    And sat upon the floor.

All that was left us
    Was a chair we couldn't break,
And the harp with a woman's head
    Nobody would take,
    For song or pity's sake.

The night before Christmas
  I cried with the cold,
I cried myself to sleep
  Like a two-year-old.

And in the deep night
    I felt my mother rise,
And stare down upon me
    With love in her eyes.

I saw my mother sitting
   On the one good chair,
A light falling on her
   From I couldn't tell where,

Looking nineteen,
   And not a day older,
And the harp with a woman's head
   Leaned against her shoulder.

Her thin fingers, moving
   In the thin, tall strings,
Were weav-weav-weaving
   Wonderful things.

Many bright threads,
   From where I couldn't see,
Were running through the harp-strings
   Rapidly,

And gold threads whistling
   Through my mother's hand.
I saw the web grow,
   And the pattern expand.

She wove a child's jacket,
    And when it was done
She laid it on the floor
    And wove another one.

She wove a red cloak
    So regal to see,
"She's made it for a king's son,"
    I said, "and not for me."
    But I knew it was for me.

She wove a pair of breeches
    Quicker than that!
She wove a pair of boots
    And a little cocked hat.

She wove a pair of mittens,
    She wove a little blouse,
She wove all night
    In the still, cold house.

She sang as she worked,
   And the harp-strings spoke;
Her voice never faltered,
   And the thread never broke.
And when I awoke,—

There sat my mother
   With the harp against her shoulder,
Looking nineteen,
   And not a day older,

A smile about her lips,
   And a light about her head,
And her hands in the harp-strings
   Frozen dead.

And piled up beside her
   And toppling to the skies,
Were the clothes of a king's son,
   Just my size.